Inside the Writing Traits Classroom

K–2 LESSONS ON DVD

RUTH CULHAM

SCHOLASTIC

New York • Toronto • London • Auckland • Sydney
Mexico City • New Delhi • Hong Kong • Buenos Aires

Acknowledgments

With sincere appreciation to the students, teachers, staff, and parents at Council Rock Primary School, Brighton School District, Rochester, New York. Remember how you laughed when we told you that the filming project would create chaos? Thanks for your flexibility, your good will, and the continued laughter when chaos was, indeed, the word of the day.

Credits:

Page 14: text and jacket cover from *The Jacket I Wear in the Snow* by Shirley Neitzel, illustrated by Nancy Winslow Parker. Text copyright © 1989 by Shirley Neitzel. Illustrations copyright © 1989 by Nancy Winslow Parker. Used by permission of Greenwillow Books, an imprint of HarperCollins.

Page 22: text and jacket cover from *Fancy Nancy* by Jane O'Connor, illustrated by Robin Preiss Glasser. Text copyright © 2006 by Jane O'Connor. Illustrations copyright © 2006 by Robin Preiss Glasser. Used by permission of HarperCollins Children's Books.

Page 26: text and jacket cover from *Hailstones and Halibut Bones* by Mary O'Neill and Leonard Weisgard, illustrator. Copyright © 1962 by Mary LeDuc O'Neill. Used by permission of Random House Children's Books, a division of Random House, Inc.

Editor: Raymond Coutu
Video production by TGF Productions, Tim Findlay, producer and editor
Cover design by Maria Lilja
Interior design by Holly Grundon
Photos by Tim Findlay
Copy Editor: Ellen Tarlin

ISBN-13: 978-0-545-04639-8
ISBN-10: 0-545-04639-4
Copyright © 2008 by Ruth Culham

Contents

Introduction

In these exciting lessons, kindergarten, first-grade, and second-grade students use the power of the traits to improve their writing. You'll find a lesson each for ideas, organization, voice, word choice, sentence fluency, and presentation on the DVD and in this guide, plus a bonus lesson on conventions in the guide.

You know better than anyone that working with primary students can be messy. Holding their attention, keeping them on task, and moving them forward is a challenge. Because these lessons were filmed during writing time in real classrooms, the authenticity shows. You'll see how master teachers at Council Rock Primary School in Brighton, New York, use the traits to structure and carry out their lessons, breaking writing down for students so they know what to do and how to do it.

* Ideas: Cathy Hutter's students explore using writer's notebooks as a way to arrive at ideas for writing.

* Organization: Paula Tantillo's students learn about logical organization for writing by thinking about the logical order of putting on snow clothing.

* Voice: Cathy Hutter's students play a game called "Whose Voice Is It?" to recognize variations in voice.

* Word Choice: Lura Kelly's students discuss the importance of using "fancy" words, or sophisticated words, in writing, using a mentor text for inspiration.

* Sentence Fluency: Jamie Bozek's students listen for sentence fluency in poetry.

* Presentation: Nita Fiore's students publish and share their writing after proofreading it against The Cinderella Checklist.

The energy and enthusiasm these teachers bring to the writing classroom is contagious—you'll see it in the children as they respond joyfully to the lessons and celebrate their successes.

This guide provides plans for the lessons featured on the 30-minute DVD, plus a bonus plan for a lesson on conventions. Included are all the materials you need for conducting these lessons with your students—step-by-step instructions, reproducible forms, children's book suggestions, and so forth, along with the scoring guides and key qualities for all seven traits.

You may want a copy of my book *6+1 Traits of Writing: The Complete Guide for the Primary Grades* (Scholastic, 2005) since it contains core information from which many of these lessons were derived, along with in-depth descriptions of the traits, scoring guides with sample student papers, conference comments, activities, and more lessons. My book *Reproducible Forms for the Writing Traits Classroom: K–2* (Scholastic, 2006) may also be useful to you. Finally, consider viewing the complete video series *Traits of Writing for the Primary Grades: A Professional Development Series on DVD* (Scholastic, 2007), which features the same K–2 teachers shown on this DVD, to see trait-specific assessment and instruction in action.

Some Background
on the Teachers

Cathy, Paula, Lura, Jamie, and Nita are members of the professional
study group at Council Rock Primary School who meet monthly
to boost their understanding of the trait model and discuss ways to
implement it effectively, with the help of literacy specialist Libby Jachles.
To prepare for the filming of this video, they read *6+1 Traits of Writing:
The Complete Guide for the Primary Grades* (Scholastic, 2005), practiced
assessing papers for each trait, and created lessons. What you see here is
the result: specific, trait-based lessons designed to support young writers
as they learn how to draft, revise, edit, and publish their work.

These teachers have learned firsthand how critical it is to understand
primary writing from the inside out. Specifically, they have learned how
to apply assessment and then design targeted lessons and activities to

develop writing skills. This two-pronged approach not only produces strong and independent primary writers, but also saves those teachers time, a definite bonus.

In their classrooms, learning how to write well is no longer a mysterious process. I can say that with confidence because I've had the privilege of visiting those classrooms. Because the teachers have dedicated time and energy to learning about and implementing the traits of writing model, the skill and confidence of their young writers soar. As a team, they have learned that writing is a powerful way to communicate ideas, document learning, and develop critical-thinking skills. Whether they're modeling a craft technique, using picture books to show examples of strong writing, or offering activities designed to teach a specific writing skill, the teachers show exactly how they inspire students to reach new heights.

Some Background on the Traits of Writing

The trait model is more than an approach to assessing and teaching writing. It's a vocabulary teachers use to describe their vision of what good writing—any kind of writing—looks like. The model is rooted in writing research, writing pedagogy, and the combined wisdom of thousands of teachers of the past 20 years.

First developed during the mid-1980s by pioneering teachers in Beaverton, Oregon, and Missoula, Montana, the traits were nurtured and expanded during the 1990s at Northwest Regional Educational Laboratory (NWREL) in Portland, Oregon. Now the traits are the focus of study and work by teachers, teacher researchers, staff developers, and consultants across the country and the world. For more history on the research and development of the trait model, see Chapter 1 of *6+1 Traits of Writing: The Complete Guide for Grades 3 and Up* by Ruth Culham (Scholastic, 2003). Or, contact www.nwrel.org for copies of additional research and historical documentation of the model.

During the 1990s, my colleagues at NWREL and I began to explore the traits of writing in the primary grades and develop criteria for assessing primary students' work. After years of studying and implementing the scoring guide for grades 3 and up, we drafted a scoring guide specifically for primary writers. We scoured the research and haunted primary classrooms asking, "What happens when primary students learn to write? What do they do first? What comes next? What evidence can we gather that important learning has occurred?" Now, more than ten years and numerous revisions later, that scoring guide and those anchor papers are the centerpiece for the textbook *6+1 Traits of Writing: The Complete Guide for the Primary Grades.*

The language of the traits is a core element in the writing classrooms of many primary teachers across the country. (For a list of each trait's key qualities, see pages 39–41.) Those teachers understand how important it is to honor the early works of young writers—those approximations of alphabet letters, attempts at words, and sketchy drawings. As students mature, they learn to add details to their drawings, to turn letters into words, and to turn words into phrases, and eventually they begin to write sentences and use conventions correctly.

This progression of skills is captured clearly on the scoring guides for primary writers, which appear on pages 42–48. Students at all stages are represented in the guides, even those who are doing little more than creating random scribbles at the "ready to begin" level. As those students develop as writers, they are able to write several sentences on the same topic, with clarity, precision, and voice. When they reach this point, they are ready to have their work assessed against the more sophisticated scoring guide intended for older writers found in *6+1 Traits of Writing: The Complete Guide for Grades 3 and Up.*

The primary scoring guide's level of detail, the ready-to-use trait-specific lessons and activities, and the thoughtful discussion of how primary writers learn to create text is why *6+1 Traits of Writing: The Complete Guide for the Primary Grades* has been welcomed and well-received by teachers everywhere. In this DVD and in the complete DVD series, we've tried to bring that book to life, showing how primary students use the traits to become better writers, with the help of their amazing and talented teachers.

Principles for Creating Confident, Capable Young Writers

This DVD is based on three core principles of teaching writing in a trait-based classroom:

We Must Speak a Common Language in All Grades
Respond to primary writing holistically and according to individual traits, using the same language from day to day and year to year in order to develop a foundation for writing assessment and instruction.

We Must Nurture Process Learning
Value process over product, in a classroom where writing is encouraged and celebrated every day.

We Must Use Criteria to Set the Standard
Use criteria, or clear indicators, to describe what we believe students must learn and to measure how well they're doing.

For additional information on using the traits with primary writers in a process-oriented writing classroom, refer to Chapters 1 and 2 in *6+1 Traits of Writing: The Complete Guide for the Primary Grades*.

Concluding Thought

All set? I hope you enjoy watching these lessons as much as the students and teachers did creating them. My sincere thanks to the forward-thinking teachers and administrators at Council Rock Primary School for letting us film their adventure and share it with others. We also want to thank the families who so graciously allowed us to capture the magic of their children's first years of formal writing instruction.

Using the Writer's Notebook

Grade shown on the DVD: First

Time: 4 minutes

Materials

❈ overhead transparency of the Writer's Notebook Pages reproducible (page 12)

❈ photocopies of the Seed Idea Notebook Cover reproducible (page 13)

❈ photocopies of the Writer's Notebook Pages. To create the notebooks, staple together the cover, the labeled pages, and two blank pages for each labeled page.

❈ paper and pencils

Lesson Focus

First-grade students learn how their teacher, Cathy Hutter, uses a writer's notebook to think about and capture possible ideas for writing. She invites students to brainstorm possible topics for their own writer's notebooks and gives each student a Seed Idea Notebook to jot down and/or draw potential ideas.

Lesson Description

1. Show students a page of your writer's notebook. If you wish, you can use an overhead of the reproducible on page 12, filling in the four sections using words, phrases, questions, pictures, and lists to capture ideas for writing. Emphasize that taking the time to enter even the quickest notation can help us remember a good idea.

2. Hand out a copy of the Seed Idea Notebook to each student. Tell students that this is what they will use as their own writer's notebook. Discuss why it is called Seed Idea Notebook and that you hope they will use it to let writing ideas grow. Students can personalize the cover by coloring in the picture and adding their own words and art.

3. Ask students to capture three ideas in their notebooks, reminding them that they can use words, phrases, questions, pictures, and/or lists. They need to write down only enough to retain the idea for consideration later.

4. Ask students to choose one of the three ideas as the topic for a piece of writing. They may wish to discuss their choice with a neighbor. Give them paper and pencils, and let them start to work.

Lesson **Extension**

1. Stress that writer's notebooks are highly individual, so no two should look exactly alike.

2. After students have used their notebooks over a period of time, have them review the contents and talk with a partner about possible writing topics.

3. Ask members of the class to share their notebook entries and resulting pieces of writing. Stress how the seed idea in the notebook leads to a longer piece of writing.

4. Every two weeks, or as time allows, ask students to share why ideas in their notebooks are special. As one student shares, another may get a new idea to include in his or her notebook.

Additional **Resource**

Read *Amelia's Notebook* by Marissa Moss, a clever picture book that shows students the range of items and entries that might find their way into a writer's notebook. It provides a concrete example of how a notebook helps a writer find good ideas.

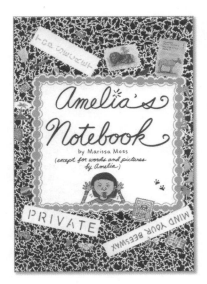

Writer's Notebook Pages

Things I notice:

Things I wonder about:

Things that make me laugh:

Things that worry me:

Seed Idea Notebook Cover

Seed Idea Notebook

_____

Writer's name

Seed Idea Notebook

_____

Writer's name

Seed Idea Notebook

_____

Writer's name

Seed Idea Notebook

_____

Writer's name

Discovering the Logical Order

**Grade shown on the DVD:
Kindergarten**

**Time:
4 minutes**

Materials

❈ copies of picture books with clear organizational structures, such as *Today Is Monday* by Eric Carle, *The Paperboy* by Dav Pilkey, *Alphabet Under Construction* by Denise Fleming, *The Snowman* by Raymond Briggs, and *The Very Hungry Caterpillar* by Eric Carle

❈ a copy of *The Jacket I Wear in the Snow* by Shirley Neitzel

❈ cutouts of clothing articles depicted in *The Jacket I Wear in the Snow*: boots, socks, sweater, jeans, cap, mittens, zipper, snowpants, jacket, and scarf. Or, if you prefer, use real articles of clothing.

❈ a string to hang across the classroom, paper clips

❈ two pairs of snow boots, two pairs of snowpants

❈ drawing paper, pens, pencils, crayons, markers

❈ scissors and glue

❈ photocopies of The Life of an Apple reproducible (page 17)

Lesson **Focus**

Kindergarten students explore the organization trait by listening to *The Jacket I Wear in the Snow* and then hanging cutout clothing articles on a string in the order in which they are mentioned in the book: first the jacket, then the scarf, then the cap, and so forth. Next, students try to put on real clothing articles the wrong way—boots before snowpants—to appreciate the importance of logical order. Finally, they put mixed-up pages from familiar books in the correct order, based on their knowledge of the organization of those books.

Lesson **Description**

1. In the weeks prior to this lesson, read and discuss the organization of various picture books such as:
   ❊ *Today Is Monday* by Eric Carle (Sunday to Saturday)

   ❊ *The Paperboy* by Dav Pilkey (morning to night)

   ❊ *Alphabet Under Construction* by Denise Fleming (A to Z)

   ❊ *The Snowman* by Raymond Briggs (sunset to sunrise)

   ❊ *The Very Hungry Caterpillar* by Eric Carle (birth to death)

2. Read and discuss the organization of *The Jacket I Wear in the Snow* by Shirley Neitzel.

3. Distribute the cutouts of clothing articles (or real articles if you wish) and ask students to help you put them in order on the string as they appeared in the book. Start by asking students where the jacket would go—at the beginning, middle, or end? Clip each article onto the string.

4. Once you've finished hanging the cutouts, ask students whether the order of the cutouts on the string represents the order in which they would actually dress themselves if they were going out in the snow.

5. Choose two students to provide a demonstration. Give each student a pair of boots to slip on first. Then hand each one a pair of snowpants to put on. Students will struggle since it's difficult to put snowpants over boots. They will likely want to reverse the order because it makes more sense and makes the task easier.

6. Ask the class to help you put the articles on the string in a more sensible order than the one shown in the book. Help students understand that some of the articles should be put before others, but some, such as mittens and hats, can be put on at any time.

7. Put students into groups of three or four. Give each group photocopied pages from another book they have read and discussed. Ask them to put the pages in order and discuss the organizational structure the author used, for example:

   ❊ *Today Is Monday* by Eric Carle (Sunday to Saturday)

   ❊ *The Paperboy* by Dav Pilkey (morning to night)

* *Alphabet Under Construction* by Denise Fleming (A to Z)

* *The Snowman* by Raymond Briggs (sunset to sunrise)

* *The Very Hungry Caterpillar* by Eric Carle (birth to death)

Lesson **Extension**

1. Put students in pairs and ask them to cut out the pictures from The Life of an Apple reproducible on page 17.

2. Fold drawing paper into four parts and number each quarter (1. top left, 2. top right, 3. bottom left, 4. bottom right) and ask students to paste the pictures in the correct box.

3. Ask students to cut out the labels (*first, next, then, finally*) and glue them under the appropriate picture. It's okay for students to use the words *next* and *then* interchangeably.

4. Share completed pieces with the whole class. Ask students whether it makes a difference which label was used and, if so, why.

5. Discuss the importance of putting details in order in writing.

6. Ask students to select another process and draw pictures with labels that show steps or stages in the process:

    * getting ready for school

    * making a sandwich

    * watching a tadpole turn into a frog

    * playing a game

    * washing your hands

Additional **Resource**

Show students the book *Scaredy Squirrel* by Mélanie Watt and point out all the different forms of writing it contains: a list, a comparison-and-contrast chart, a schedule, a table of contents, and so on. Ask students to select one form and create their own piece of writing.

The Life of an Apple

next   first   finally   then

Recognizing Voice

Grade shown on the DVD: First	**Materials**
	❊ overhead transparency of the Sentences With Voice reproducible (page 20)
Time: 3 minutes	❊ photocopies of the Choices of Voices reproducible (page 21)

Lesson **Focus**

First-grade students close their eyes, listen to the sound of classmates' voices, and try to guess who is speaking. They talk about qualities that characterize each speaking voice and the importance of having similar qualities in their writing voices.

Lesson **Description**

1. Explain to students that they are going to play a game to help them learn about the voice trait. While their eyes are closed, they will listen to a classmate say, "Hello, everybody," and then try to identify that classmate.

2. Arrange the students in a large circle, facing outward, and ask them to close their eyes

3. From inside the circle, quietly tap a student on the shoulder and ask him or her to say, "Hello, everybody."

4. Ask students to open their eyes and raise their hands if they think they know whose voice they heard.

5. Let students guess until someone gives the correct answer.

6. Have students close their eyes again, select another student to say, "Hello, everybody," and repeat steps 4 and 5.

7. Continue choosing students to speak and letting the class guess for as long as time allows.

8. Ask students to face inward and discuss how they recognized each classmate's voice. Remind students that speaking voices are distinctly individual, as are writing voices. Let them know that you are going to help them develop strong writing voices in this next part of the lesson.

Lesson **Extension**

1. Make an overhead and, if you wish, a photocopy for each student of the Sentences With Voice reproducible on page 20.

2. Give each student a photocopy of the Choices of Voices reproducible on page 21.

3. Read the first sentence from the overhead. Ask students to use their Choices of Voices word bank to select the adjective that matches the voice to the sentence. Write the selected word next to the sentence on the overhead.

4. After you have covered all five sentences, ask students to pair up and select one sentence from the overhead, write it out on the Choices of Voices sheet, and add two or three more sentences to expand the idea, keeping the voice consistent with the first sentence.

5. When all students have finished, ask volunteers to share their writing. Some pairs will have selected the same sentence as others, so it will be interesting to see variations in their approaches.

6. Post the Choices of Voices word bank on a bulletin board so that all students can refer to it as they write. Add new words that describe different voices as you and the class discover them.

Additional **Resource**

Share some of the poems from *Bugs: Poems About Creeping Things* by David L. Harrison and illustrated by Rob Shepperson. Ask students to identify the voice in each poem—there is a range, from scary to silly. Add new words that describe voice to the Choices of Voices word bank on the bulletin board.

Sentences With Voice

1. I noticed that the back door was open at about the same time I noticed that my new puppy was missing.

2. I'd been counting the days until my birthday and it was finally here!

3. No matter how hard I tried, I just couldn't whistle.

4. Just thinking about my grandpa makes me smile.

5. The way my sister snorts when she laughs always cracks me up.

Word Bank

scared	sweet	nervous
comical	excited	happy
discouraged	upset	kind
silly	thoughtful	funny
frustrated	worried	delighted

Inside the Writing Traits Classroom © 2008 by Ruth Culham, Scholastic

Choices of Voices

scared	sweet	nervous
comical	excited	happy
discouraged	upset	kind
silly	thoughtful	funny
frustrated	worried	delighted

Write the sentence of your choice from the lesson and circle the word(s) that gives it voice. Then add two or three more sentences of your own, keeping the voice the same throughout.

_____

_____

_____

_____

_____

_____

_____

Inside the Writing Traits Classroom © 2008 by Ruth Culham, Scholastic

Choosing "Fancy" Words

Grade shown on the DVD: First	**Materials**
	❋ a copy of *Fancy Nancy* by Jane O'Connor
	❋ chart paper and markers
Time: 4 minutes	❋ photocopies of the "Plain" Words List reproducible (page 24)
	❋ photocopies of the "Fancy" Words List reproducible (page 25)

Lesson **Focus**

First-grade students experience the delightful book *Fancy Nancy*, in which Nancy, the main character, prides herself for using only fancy-sounding words such as *plume*, *parfait*, and *chauffeur*. Throughout the book, Nancy explains why she likes the fancy versions of words more than the ordinary versions. In the lesson, students get a chance to look closely at Nancy's word choices and then try their hand at using fancy words of their own.

Lesson **Description**

1. Share *Fancy Nancy* with students, pausing to point out some of the more interesting words as you read.

2. On the chart paper, make a list of the "fancy" words from the text: *fuchsia, plume, stupendous, accessories, posh, chauffeur, parfaits,* and *dressing gown*.

3. Ask students to tell you what the fancy words mean in plain English and then write their responses next to each word. Encourage students to use the story context to guess the meaning of the fancy words if students are not familiar with them.

4. Discuss why authors are careful about choosing just-right words and how those words make the ideas more interesting.

Lesson **Extension**

1. Make photocopies of the "Fancy" Words List and "Plain" Words List on pages 24 and 25. Cut them apart so that single words are on individual strips.

2. Divide the class in half. Give one "fancy" word strip to each student in one group. Give a "plain" word strip to each student in the other group.

3. Tell students that they have two minutes to find their word's partner. They should move around the room, calling out their word until they find a match. If students with "fancy" words ask for help, consult the master list below and give them synonyms to help them figure out the meaning of their word.

bad: ghastly	good: delightful
happy: blissful	blue: turquoise
sad: gloomy	run: gallop
pretty: glamorous	big: enormous
cool: marvelous	fast: swift
lazy: sluggish	hard: challenging
nice: pleasing	walk: stroll

4. When students have found their matching word, ask them to sit down so that they don't distract others who are continuing to look.

5. Once all the students have found their matching word, ask them to come up in pairs to record their words on the chart paper under the headings "fancy" and "plain."

6. Ask the class if it had any favorite "fancy" words, and, if so, encourage students to write them in their writer's notebooks to use in their own writing later.

Additional **Resource**

Students may enjoy hearing you read *The Boy Who Loved Words* by Roni Schotter, in which the main character, like Nancy, enjoys collecting words. Have the class develop its own lists of favorite words after reading this delightful story.

"Plain" Words List

bad	happy
sad	blue
run	pretty
big	good
cool	fast
lazy	hard
nice	walk

Inside the Writing Traits Classroom © 2008 by Ruth Culham, Scholastic

"Fancy" Words List

ghastly	blissful
gloomy	turquoise
gallop	glamorous
enormous	delightful
marvelous	swift
sluggish	challenging
pleasing	stroll

Becoming Fluent With Poetry

Grade shown on the DVD: First

Time: 3 minutes

Materials

❋ a copy of *Hailstones and Halibut Bones* by Mary O'Neill

❋ chart paper with O'Neill's poem "What Is Green?" written on it

❋ photocopies of the Fun With Sentences reproducible (page 29)

Lesson **Focus**

Second graders listen to their teacher, Jamie Bozek, read aloud the poem "What Is Green?" which contains carefully chosen words in just the right places, producing rhythm and flow, all of which makes it easy on the ear. Jamie and the students then discuss the importance of sentence fluency in both poetry and prose. In the second half of the lesson, students try changing sentence beginnings and lengths in their own writing to create fluency.

Lesson **Description**

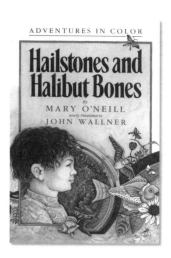

1. Discuss sentence fluency with students, emphasizing that it is the auditory trait. So when writers apply the trait, they think about the lengths of their sentences, the beginnings and endings of their sentences, how the words and phrases within their sentences sound, and how their sentences sound when they're strung together. Tell students that you will be reading aloud a poem and ask them to listen closely for fluency.

2. Read "What Is Green?" a poem from the collection *Hailstones and Halibut Bones*. Take your time reading, emphasizing O'Neill's beautiful phrasing.

Enjoy yourself. When you're finished, ask students:

- Did you think this piece was fluent?

- What did the writer do to make it sound good?

- What image or phrase stood out for you?

3. Show students the poem on the chart paper and ask them, Where is your favorite image or phrase? At the beginning of a line? At the end? In the middle?

4. Remind students that being fluent means writing sentences that do not all sound alike. Give them an example of a piece of writing with sentences that begin the same way and are the same length:

My dog is big.

My dog is red.

My dog is funny.

My dog smells.

Ask students to help you make one or more of these sentences more fluent. They might combine two or three sentences into one, or they might try a new sentence beginning: "My big, red dog smells funny." "My dog is funny and he smells." "It's funny to watch my big, red dog."

5. Write their revisions on the board or chart to illustrate how to make bland, boring sentences sound more interesting.

Lesson Extension

1. Tell students that you are going to create a piece of writing together. Write the first sentence on the board or overhead, such as: "When I wake up in the morning, I'm excited to come to school," and then ask one of them to give you the next sentence. And here's the fun part: Their new sentence must begin with the last word of the first sentence. For example: "School is a fun place to play and learn." (You can use a form of the word if it makes it easier for students, and for you!)

2. Alternate between you and the students, until you have several sentences to look at together. Distribute photocopies of the Fun With Sentences reproducible on page 29, so that students can record the sentences as you go, too.

Here's an example of how the piece I started above might continue:

Teacher: Learning how to write is hard, but <u>important</u>.

Students: <u>Important</u> things are learned at school every <u>day</u>.

Teacher: <u>Days</u> fly by when you teach <u>second graders</u>.

Students: <u>Second graders</u> are the best writers in the school.

3. Discuss with students the importance of varying sentence lengths and beginnings to create fluent writing. Remind them to check for this in their own work as they draft and to help their writing partners with it, too.

Additional **Resource**

Read aloud the picture book *Yesterday I Had the Blues* by Jeron Ashford Frame. Frame's prose reads like poetry. Point out to students that Frame achieves this, to a large degree, by varying the beginnings and lengths of his sentences. Ask students to compare how Frame and Mary O'Neill create fluency.

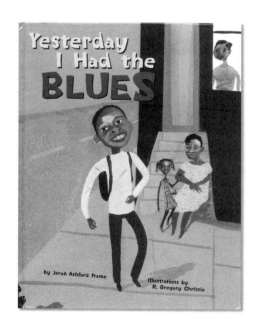

Fun With Sentences

Write down your teacher's sentence in the first line. Then start each new sentence with the last word of the sentence before it. Writing sentences that begin differently from one another can make your work sound smooth and interesting.

Teacher: _____ .

Students: _____ .

Teacher: _____ .

Students: _____ .

Teacher: _____ .

Students: _____ .

Teacher: _____ .

Students: _____ .

PRESENTATION

"Getting Cinderella Ready for the Ball"

**Grade shown on the DVD:
First**

**Time:
4 minutes**

Materials

❋ photocopies and an overhead transparency of The Cinderella Checklist reproducible (page 32)

❋ chart paper and markers

❋ student papers

Lesson **Focus**

First-grade teacher Nita Fiore introduces her students to The Cinderella Checklist, a tool to help her students create polished, finished pieces of writing. Students select a piece of writing they'd like to publish and use the checklist to make sure it is ready to share. Then they take turns sharing their writing in the author's chair, showing the audience each page, which has been so carefully and neatly written.

Lesson **Description**

1. Distribute copies of The Cinderella Checklist and display it on the overhead.

2. Go over each step with students, reminding them that it's important to make their final copy neat, inviting, and easy to read so that the reader can enjoy it.

3. Ask students to select a piece of their writing that is ready to publish. Using The Cinderella Checklist as a guide, have them recopy their work.

4. When they're finished, ask for volunteers to share their writing. After each student shares, note positive qualities of the writing and wise ways he or she has applied The Cinderella Checklist.

Lesson **Extension**

1. Give students time to look through picture books for features used by the authors and illustrators, such as variations in type style and size, speech bubbles, and interesting use of color, photographs, and illustrations.

2. As a class, make a list of the features and ask students to think about the purpose of each one. Your list might wind up looking something like this:

   ❊ Extra-large letters and words: to show emphasis

   ❊ Speech bubbles: to bring voice to the characters

   ❊ Interesting use of color: to catch the eye and make a page or part of a page stand out

   ❊ Photographs: to make the idea seem more realistic

   ❊ Type style: to make the text visually appealing. (For example, a handwriting font might make the narrator seem more human.)

   ❊ Art media: to set a tone for the text. (For example, watercolors might set a soft and gentle tone, whereas acrylics might set an exciting and energetic tone.)

3. Discuss how the features might help the reader understand and/or enjoy the book.

4. Ask students to pick a book with a presentation they like and, in small groups, discuss the features the author and illustrator employ that attract students to the text.

5. Encourage students to refer to the books and the list for ideas to make their own writing more interesting and inviting.

Additional **Resource**

Go to www.hhmi.org/coolscience. Ask students to name the different visual elements that appear on the home page: Go buttons, pictures, headings, descriptive text, links to other pages, search box, and so on. Divide the class into small groups; give each group paper, pens, pencils, and markers; and ask them to draw and write headings for a home page on a science topic of their choice, such as frogs, stars, tornadoes, or rocks. Encourage students to include visual elements from the example you provided.

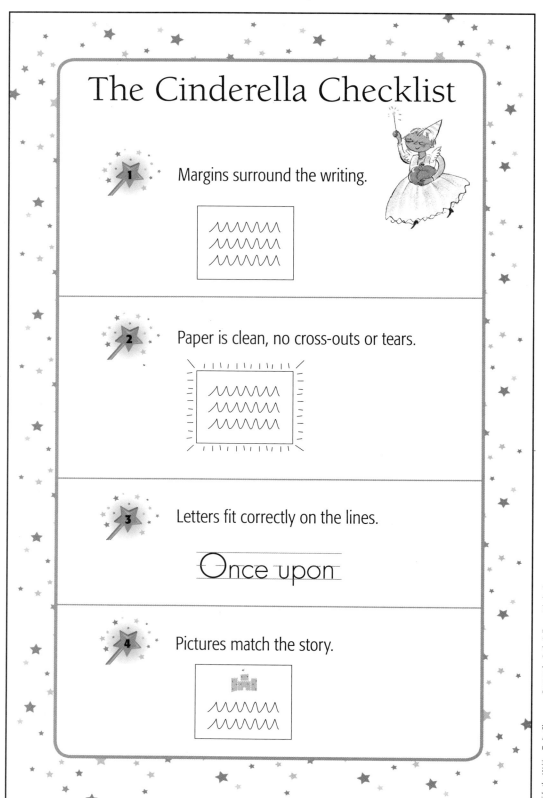

The Cinderella Checklist

1 Margins surround the writing.

2 Paper is clean, no cross-outs or tears.

3 Letters fit correctly on the lines.

Once upon

4 Pictures match the story.

Inside the Writing Traits Classroom © 2008 by Ruth Culham, Scholastic

Working With End Punctuation

Not shown on the DVD

Grade levels: K–2

Materials

* ❋ picture books containing a variety of end punctuation marks—one book for every two students in your class

* ❋ sticky notes

* ❋ paper, pencils, pens, markers

* ❋ photocopies of the Using End Punctuation Marks reproducible (page 36)

Lesson **Focus**

Working in pairs, students learn to make good editing decisions by exploring how authors use end punctuation (periods, exclamation marks, and question marks) in picture books. They put sticky notes on pages where more than one type of punctuation mark is used, such as a period and a question mark, an exclamation mark and a period, or a question mark and an exclamation mark. Then they share their findings with other students. The class discusses how often exclamation marks and question marks are used, compared to periods. Then students write sentences that require various kinds of end punctuation.

Lesson **Description**

1. Put students in pairs and give each pair a picture book of your choice.

2. Ask students to look through the book and notice each sentence's end punctuation.

3. Determine with the class the three most common types of marks—most likely periods, question marks, and exclamation marks. Write the name of each mark on the board or overhead and ask students to help you determine the purpose of each one. Your list might look something like this:

.	Period to mark the end of a declarative statement
?	Question mark to show a question being asked
!	Exclamation mark to show a command or high emotion such as surprise, joy, or fear

4. Tell students to go through their books and flag with sticky notes any page where two or more different end punctuation marks are used, such as periods and a question mark, periods and an exclamation mark, or a question mark and an exclamation mark. Ask them to write the end punctuation marks from that page on the note.

5. When they're finished, have them exchange books with another pair to make sure all the pages with two different marks are accounted for.

6. Discuss what students have noticed. Ask: Which end punctuation mark was used most frequently?

7. Explain that periods are used most often because they are used to show the end of a declarative statement, the most common type of sentence. Question marks and exclamation marks are used less frequently.

Inside the Writing Traits Classroom

Lesson **Extension**

1. Ask students to work with their partners to create three sentences with *no* end punctuation: one that should end with a period; one that should end with a question mark; and one that should end with an exclamation mark, using a copy of the Using End Punctuation Marks reproducible on page 36.

2. Have partners exchange their sentences with another pair of students in order to fill in the boxes with the correct end punctuation marks. Encourage students to read the sentences aloud to hear how question marks and exclamation marks affect their inflection. Have pairs check each other's answers for accuracy.

Additional **Resource**

Read to students Gary Paulsen's extremely well-written *Dogteam*, showing them the pages as you go. When you finish, go back through the pages and have students help you record on chart paper or the overhead all the different punctuation marks that Paulsen uses to make his text read smoothly: commas, periods, hyphens, semicolons, question marks, ellipses. Students may not know the name or purpose of some of these marks, so be prepared to explain them and invite students to try using them in their own writing.

GARY PAULSEN

Dogteam

illustrated by Ruth Wright Paulsen

Using End Punctuation Marks

Write three sentences below: one that requires a period, one that requires a question mark, and one that requires an exclamation mark at the end. But don't write those marks. Instead, share your sentences with a pair of classmates and let them fill in the marks in the boxes.

| Hint |

Mix up the order of your sentences so that your classmates don't know which mark to use unless they read the sentence carefully.

1. _____

_____

_____ ☐

2. _____

_____

_____ ☐

3. _____

_____

_____ ☐

Inside the Writing Traits Classroom © 2008 by Ruth Culham, Scholastic

References

PROFESSIONAL RESOURCES CITED

Culham, R. (2003). *6+1 Traits of Writing: The Complete Guide for Grades 3 and Up*. New York: Scholastic.

Culham, R. (2005). *6+1 Traits of Writing: The Complete Guide for the Primary Grades*. New York: Scholastic.

Culham, R. (2006). *Reproducible Forms for the Writing Traits Classroom: K–2*. New York: Scholastic.

Culham, R. (2007). *Traits of Writing for the Primary Grades: A Professional Development Video Series on DVD*. New York: Scholastic.

CHILDREN'S BOOKS CITED

Briggs, R. (1978). *The Snowman*. New York: Random House.

Carle, E. (1993). *Today Is Monday*. New York: Philomel Books.

Carle, E. (1979). *The Very Hungry Caterpillar*. New York: Philomel Books.

Fleming, D. (2002). *Alphabet Under Construction*. New York: Henry Holt.

Frame, J. (2003). *Yesterday I Had the Blues*. Berkeley, CA: Tricycle Press.

Harrison, D. (2007). *Bugs: Poems About Creepy Things*. Honesdale, PA: Wordsong.

Moss, M. (1995). *Amelia's Notebook*. Berkeley, CA: Tricycle Press.

Neitzel, S. (1989). *The Jacket I Wear in the Snow*. New York: Greenwillow Books.

O'Connor, J. (2006). *Fancy Nancy*. New York: HarperCollins.

O'Neill, M. (1961). *Hailstones and Halibut Bones: Adventures in Color*. Garden City, NY: Doubleday.

Paulsen, G. (1993). *Dogteam*. New York: Delacorte Press.

Pilkey, D. (1996). *The Paperboy*. New York: Orchard Books.

Schotter, R. (2006). *The Boy Who Loved Words*. New York: Schwartz & Wade Books.

Watt, M. (2006). *Scaredy Squirrel*. Tonawanda, NY: Kids Can Press Ltd.

Appendices

Key Qualities of Each Trait

pages 39–41

Scoring Guides for Each Trait

pages 42–48

Key Qualities
of the Ideas Trait

Interesting topic

Meaningful details

Fully developed thoughts

Narrowed focus

Key Qualities
of the Organization Trait

A brilliant beginning

A mighty middle

An excellent ending

Well-ordered details

Key Qualities
of the Voice Trait

Writing sounds like the writer.

Writer and reader connect.

Writing has energy and sparkle.

Writer is excited about the topic.

Key Qualities
of the Word Choice Trait

Just-right words and phrases

Picturesque descriptions

Fresh and original expressions

Colorful, interesting, and snappy words

Inside the Writing Traits Classroom © 2008 by Ruth Culham, Scholastic

Key Qualities
of the Sentence Fluency Trait

Sentences that sound smooth

Sentences that are well built

Sentences that have differing lengths

Sentences that have varied constructions

Key Qualities
of the Conventions and Presentation Traits

Correct spelling

Correct use of capitals

Correct use of punctuation

Well-edited text

Neat and inviting look

Ready to move to the grades-3-and-up scoring guide!

The Primary Scoring Guide
Ideas

Established
5
_____ The idea is clear and coherent.
_____ The text is a well-developed paragraph.
_____ Elaboration through interesting details creates meaning for the reader.

_____ The writer shows understanding of the topic through personal experience or research.
_____ Pictures (if present) enhance the key ideas but aren't necessary for comprehension.

Extending
4
_____ The writing works by itself to explain a simple idea or story.
_____ The writing is made up of several sentences on one topic.
_____ Key details begin to surface.

_____ The writing makes sense, but some information may be missing or irrelevant.
_____ Pictures and text work harmoniously to create a rich treatment of the topic.

Expanding
3
_____ The idea is written in a basic sentence.
_____ A simple statement with somewhat detailed pictures captures the topic.

_____ Basic details are present in the text; the illustrations work to enhance the main idea.
_____ The text contains real words.
_____ Text and pictures are understandable to the reader.

Exploring
2
_____ One or more ideas are present in the most general way.
_____ Letters and words can be picked out as clues to the topic.
_____ The drawing helps to clarify the idea.

_____ The text is composed of simple, recognizable letters with some early attempts at words.
_____ The reader gets the basic idea but needs the writer's assistance to comprehend it fully.

Ready to Begin
1
_____ The piece conveys little meaning.
_____ Real-life objects show up in drawings.
_____ Drawings may not be completely recognizable.

_____ Letters are not consistent or standard.
_____ An oral reading by the writer is needed to understand the message.

Inside the Writing Traits Classroom © 2008 by Ruth Culham, Scholastic

Inside the Writing Traits Classroom © 2008 by Ruth Culham, Scholastic

Ready to move to the grades-3-and-up scoring guide!

The Primary Scoring Guide
Organization

Established
5

_____ The title (if present) is thoughtful and effective.

_____ There is a clear beginning, middle, and end.

_____ Important ideas are highlighted within the text.

_____ Everything fits together nicely.

_____ The text slows down and speeds up to highlight the ideas and shows the writer's skill at pacing.

_____ Clear transitions connect one sentence to the next.

Extending
4

_____ The title (if present) comes close to capturing the central idea.

_____ The writing starts out strong and includes a predictable ending.

_____ The writer uses a pattern to spotlight the most important details.

_____ Ideas follow a logical but obvious sequence.

_____ The writing's pace is even; it doesn't bog the reader down.

_____ Basic transitions link one sentence to the next.

Expanding
3

_____ The simple title (if present) states the topic.

_____ The piece contains a beginning but not a conclusion.

_____ The piece is little more than a list of sentences connected by theme.

_____ There is basic order with a few missteps.

_____ There is more text at the beginning than in the middle or end.

_____ Sentence parts are linked with conjunctions (*but*, *and*, *or*).

Exploring
2

_____ The piece has no title.

_____ Letters or words are used as captions.

_____ Simple clues about order emerge in pictures or text.

_____ The arrangement of pictures or text shows an awareness of the importance of structure and pattern.

_____ Left-to-right, top-to-bottom orientation is evident.

_____ No transitions are indicated.

Ready to Begin
1

_____ Letters (if present) are scattered across the page.

_____ No coordination of written elements is evident.

_____ Lines, pictures, or letters are randomly placed on the page.

_____ Lines, pictures, or letters are grouped haphazardly.

_____ There is no sense of order.

The Primary Scoring Guide
Voice

Ready to move to the grades-3-and-up scoring guide!

Established — 5
_____ The writer "owns" the topic.
_____ The piece contains the writer's imprint.
_____ The writer is mindful of the piece's audience and connects purposefully with the reader.
_____ The tone is identifiable—bittersweet, compassionate, frustrated, terrified, and so on.
_____ The writer takes real risks, creating a truly individual piece of writing.

Extending — 4
_____ The writer takes a standard topic and addresses it in a nonstandard way.
_____ The writer tries a new word, interesting image, or unusual detail.
_____ The writing speaks to the reader in several places.
_____ The writing captures a general mood such as happy, sad, or mad.
_____ The writer begins to show how he or she really thinks and feels about the topic.

Expanding — 3
_____ There are fleeting glimpses of how the writer looks at the topic.
_____ Touches of originality are found in the text and pictures.
_____ There is a moment of audience awareness, but then it fades.
_____ BIG letters, exclamation points, underlining, repetition, and pictures are used for emphasis.
_____ A pat summary statement conceals the writer's individuality.

Exploring — 2
_____ The piece is a routine response to the assignment.
_____ The writer copies environmental text but also adds an original bit.
_____ The text connects with the reader in the most general way.
_____ The drawings begin to reveal the individual.
_____ The barest hint of the writer is in evidence.

Ready to Begin — 1
_____ The reader is not sure why the writer chose this idea for writing.
_____ The writer tries to copy without purpose what he or she sees around the room.
_____ No awareness of audience is evident.
_____ The piece contains very simple drawings or lines.
_____ Nothing distinguishes the work to make it the writer's own.

Inside the Writing Traits Classroom © 2008 by Ruth Culham, Scholastic

The Primary Scoring Guide

Word Choice

Ready to move to the grades-3-and-up scoring guide!

Established — 5

_____ The writer uses everyday words and phrases with a fresh and original spin.
_____ The words paint a clear picture in the reader's mind.

_____ The writer uses just the right words or phrase.
_____ Figurative language works reasonably well.
_____ Colorful words are used correctly and with creativity.

Extending — 4

_____ Descriptive nouns (e.g., *Raisin Bran*, not *cereal*) are combined with generic ones.
_____ The writer uses an active verb or two.

_____ There is very little repetition of words.
_____ The writer attempts figurative language.
_____ The writer "stretches" by using different types of words.

Expanding — 3

_____ Some words make sense.
_____ The reader begins to see what the writer is describing.
_____ One or two words stand out.

_____ Occasional misuse of words bogs the reader down.
_____ The writer tries out new words.

Exploring — 2

_____ Conventional letters are present.
_____ The letter strings begin to form words.
_____ Letter strings can be read as words even though the spacing and spelling aren't correct.

_____ Words from the board, displays, or word walls are attempted.
_____ A few words can be identified.

Ready to Begin — 1

_____ Scribbling and random lines mark the page.
_____ Imitation letters may be present.
_____ There may be random strings of letters across the page.

_____ Writer uses his or her name.
_____ Few, if any, recognizable words are present.

Inside the Writing Traits Classroom © 2008 by Ruth Culham, Scholastic

Ready to move to the grades-3-and-up scoring guide!

The Primary Scoring Guide
Sentence Fluency

Established — 5
_____ Different sentence lengths give the writing a nice sound. There is playfulness and experimentation.
_____ Varied sentence beginnings create a pleasing rhythm.

_____ Different kinds of sentences (statements, commands, questions, and exclamations) are present.
_____ The flow from one sentence to the next is smooth.
_____ The piece is a breeze to read aloud.

Extending — 4
_____ Sentences are of different lengths.
_____ Sentences start differently.
_____ Some sentences read smoothly while others still need work.

_____ Connectives are correctly used in long and short sentences.
_____ Aside from a couple of awkward moments, the piece can be read aloud easily.

Expanding — 3
_____ Basic subject-verb agreement occurs in simple sentences— for example, "I jumped."
_____ Sentence beginnings are identical, making all sentences sound alike.
_____ Longer sentences go on and on.

_____ Simple conjunctions such as *and* and *but* are used to make compound sentences.
_____ The piece is easy to read aloud, although it may contain repetitive or awkward sentence patterns.

Exploring — 2
_____ Written elements work together in units.
_____ Words are combined to make short, repetitive phrases.
_____ Awkward word patterns break the flow of the piece.

_____ The reader gets only one or two clues about how the pictures and text are connected.
_____ The writer stumbles when reading the text aloud and may have to back up and reread.

Ready to Begin — 1
_____ It's hard to figure out how the elements go together.
_____ Words, if present, stand alone.
_____ Imitation words and letters are used across the page.

_____ There is no overall sense of flow to the piece.
_____ Only the writer can read the piece aloud.

The Primary Scoring Guide
Conventions

Ready to move to the grades-3-and-up scoring guide!

Established — 5

- _____ High-use words are spelled correctly and others are easy to read.
- _____ The writer applies basic capitalization rules with consistency.
- _____ Punctuation marks are used effectively to guide the reader.
- _____ One or more paragraphs with indenting are present.
- _____ Standard English grammar is used.
- _____ Conventions are applied consistently and accurately.

Extending — 4

- _____ Spelling is correct or close on high-use words (*kiten, saed, want*).
- _____ Sentence beginnings and proper nouns are usually capitalized.
- _____ The writer uses end punctuation and series commas correctly.
- _____ The writer may try more advanced punctuation (dashes, ellipses, quotation marks) but not always with success.
- _____ Only minor editing is required to show thoughtful use of conventions.

Expanding — 3

- _____ Spelling is inconsistent (phonetic spelling—*kitn, sed, wnt*) but readable.
- _____ Upper- and lowercase letters are used correctly.
- _____ Capitals mark the beginning of sentences.
- _____ End punctuation marks are generally used correctly.
- _____ The writing correctly follows simple conventions.

Exploring — 2

- _____ The words are unreadable to the untrained eye (quasi-phonetic spelling—*KN, sD, Wt*).
- _____ There is little discrimination between upper- and lowercase letters.
- _____ Spacing between letters and words is present.
- _____ The writer experiments with punctuation.
- _____ The use of conventions is not consistent.

Ready to Begin — 1

- _____ Letters are written in strings (prephonetic spelling—*gGmkrRt*).
- _____ Letters are formed irregularly; there is no intentional use of upper- and lowercase letters.
- _____ Spacing is uneven between letters and words.
- _____ Punctuation is not present.
- _____ The piece does not employ standard conventions.

Ready to move to the grades-3-and-up scoring guide!

The Primary Scoring Guide

Presentation

Established 5

_____ The margins frame the text for easy reading.

_____ Pictures and text look planned and work where they are placed.

_____ The handwriting is legible and consistent in form.

_____ There are no stray marks, cross-outs, or tears on the paper.

_____ The overall appearance is neat and pleasing to the eye.

Extending 4

_____ Margins are present but not consistent.

_____ White space is used effectively, but words or pictures are often jammed at the end of lines.

_____ Most letters are formed correctly and legibly.

_____ A few cross-outs and smudges mar an otherwise pleasing appearance.

_____ The overall presentation is organized with only minor distractions.

Expanding 3

_____ Margins show awareness of left-to-right/top-to-bottom directionality, though they are not evenly spaced.

_____ White space is present but inconsistent in size.

_____ The handwriting is more legible at the beginning than at the end.

_____ There are cross-outs and stray marks but only a few small smudges or tears from erasing.

_____ The piece looks rushed.

Exploring 2

_____ Attempts at margins are inconsistent.

_____ The writing contains irregular chunks of white space.

_____ Letters slant in different directions and form different shapes and sizes.

_____ Many cross-outs, marks, and tears divert attention.

_____ Only a last-minute attempt was made to create a readable piece.

Ready to Begin 1

_____ No margins are present.

_____ The use of white space is random and ineffective.

_____ The handwriting is messy and illegible.

_____ There are many cross-outs, stray marks, or tears from erasing.

_____ Little care went into this piece to make it readable or understandable.

Inside the Writing Traits Classroom © 2008 by Ruth Culham, Scholastic